MW00877623

55 Daily People Skills

Dre Baldwin

Dre Baldwin

Copyright © 2016 Work On Your Game Inc

All rights reserved.

ISBN: 1539145158
ISBN-13: 978-1539145158

DEDICATION

To the people who know you need people.

CONTENTS

INTRODUCTION

It's happened to me, too. A lack of connections has cost me opportunities.

Knowing the right people - who knew and liked me - has helped me many times as well.

It seems random, but what if we could get some control over these occurrences?

What if you could develop and strategically use skills for connecting with people? What if you could then leverage those connections to advance your interests while helping others?

This isn't "too good to be true." People are doing it, every single day.

With this book. you're next.

***

Everything you do will involve people.

In sports, you have teammates, opponents and coaches.

Businesses have co-workers, customers, prospects, suppliers, employees and bosses.

Relationships don't even exist without at least 2 people involved.

Making money, winning awards, getting jobs, getting known...all require people to be involved.

All this said, your people skills must constantly improve. Expanding your ability to deal with people will always help you.

Here, you'll learn 55 people skills that need to become part of your communication arsenal starting now. Some, you may have been taught before. Some will be completely new to you. Some you may know about, but have forgotten to remember to use. Let this be your reminder.

Avoid the mistake of thinking you "already know" anything within this book. Because *knowing* it is your problem! If you were *doing* it instead of just knowing it, you would be getting better results with people, and in turn increased success in every area of your life.

This booklet will infuse you with 55 basic, everyday-use people skills.

How soon can you start? How soon will you see results? How about the next time you communicate with a person!

Remember: Communication is much more than just talking. Read on and learn. Then **do something** with what you know.

(**Note:** Speaking with a fake smile is the same as having no smile at all. We cannot fool our or others' subconscious minds in this way.)

Smile when you speak, and notice how your communications change for the better.

3 IF YOU'RE HAPPY, MAKE SURE YOUR FACE KNOWS ABOUT IT!

I heard a speaker named Michael Hyatt once talk about how he found out about this principle.

Michael was in a leadership position in a company, and a staff meeting had just ended. One of his colleagues pulled Michael aside and asked him if he was angry about anything.

Michael said he wasn't angry at all, and wondered why she had asked.

"Well, Michael, if you're *not* angry, you might want to tell your face!"

People can be turned off, intimidated and even made to change their minds about approaching you based on your facial expression. Make sure yours isn't costing you business and opportunity.

Sometimes our "normal" facial expressions can be quite intimidating. This can be especially true if we're deep in thought or considering a tough decision. Or if you just happen to be a very determined person who's always grinding. Your default face may be saying, *Leave me alone!*

Take control of this: Assume your normal face, and take a selfie. Look at yourself in photographs. Ask the people who are around you most if you seem to be angry or bothered even when you say you're not.

You could be scaring people off.

4 ALWAYS USE *PLEASE* AND *THANK YOU*, EVEN WITH YOUR SUBORDINATES AND CHILDREN.

Manners and common courtesy and not just for children and people talking to their bosses. They are for everyone - *especially* those in leadership and power positions.

Why? Because there is never a reason to not show courtesy to other people. And yes, that includes the people whose checks you sign and the kids who live under your roof. And the front desk guy at the gym and the janitor mopping the floor.

A true measure of how big someone is can be found in how a person deals with someone who can do nothing for him, or someone who has considerably less power and influence than he.

It takes less energy to be polite than it takes to be a jerk.

You don't want to tempt the Karma gods into teaching you a lesson about how mortal you truly are, do you?

5 BE INTERESTED IN PEOPLE.

Everything you ever do on your journey to success will involve people.

The money you earn will come from **people**.

The teams you join only exists because there are other **people** involved.

A true entrepreneur doesn't do all the work herself - she enlists the resources of other **people**.

We are all narcissists at heart: we care more about ourselves than we do about anyone else. This is the way it should be.

Knowing this, you now have a secret weapon. People love when they get to indulge in their favorite things. Since everyone is interested in themselves, all you have to do is get people taking about their favorite subject. Without knowing anything about you, a person will be a huge fan of you - just because you let him talk to his heart's desire!

Have you ever been annoyed by a person who talked about themselves too much? Now you can start using it to your advantage. Let someone talk about themselves as much as he wants. You'll have a new fan.

6 ASK QUESTIONS MORE THAN YOU TALK.

You already know what peoples' favorite subject is. So start using it as an offensive weapon.

This weapon will allow you to learn more and faster.

This weapon will make you more friends.

This weapon makes other people happy, since very few people ever stay quiet long enough to listen to anyone else!

This weapon also saves you from yourself and the possibility of saying the wrong thing at the wrong time.

Ask questions. Many questions. Get good at formulating questions and learn the difference between *open* and *closed* questions. Use the former the most.

7 REMEMBER PEOPLE'S NAMES.

Your name is the sweetest sound your ears have ever known. Other people have the same affinity - for *their* names.

Once someone shares their favorite word with you, you lose a golden opportunity with them if you forget it.

Repeat a name when you hear it. Use it in conversation. *Write it down*.

Just don't forget it.

8 PAY PEOPLE GENUINE COMPLIMENTS.

Most people are good by nature. Even criminals, for the most part, do what they do to better their own situations.

So you, in dealing with the 99% of the population that are law abiding citizens, need to condition yourself to look for the good in others. It won't be hard to find.

When you find it, it's important that you let others know about the good you see. Tell him how much you appreciate his consistent effort, even if it's not producing optimal results. Tell her how much you admire her cooking ability.

Whatever compliment you choose, make sure you *mean* it and don't just say it to say it. Remember what

I told you about smiling: fake ones aren't fooling anyone.

9 BE NICE AND FRIENDLY. YOU KNOW HOW TO DO THAT.

The energy you put out is the energy you will get back. Jerks and a**holes attract the same attitudes back to them. Being friendly will bring out the friendly side in others.

Make it a habit.

10 FIND WAYS TO HELP PEOPLE AND DO IT!

Start right where you stand. - Napoleon Hill

When you see an opportunity to help other people, do it.

When you know you can do something that makes other people's day better, do it.

When you want to put people in debt to you, help them first.

When you want to increase your pay, increase your value by helping others.

When you need help, check your help bank account. How many people have you helped whom you can now call on?

11 SPEAK CLEARLY SO PEOPLE CAN HEAR YOU.

Remember that communication is more about the *how* then the *what*.

When you speak, stand up or sit straight - this helps your voice carry. Speak from your belly and pace yourself. Look people in the eye and remember to smile!

Annunciate your words. Avoid word fillers (*um, you know, ah, like, so, and, etc*).

12 LOOK INTO THE EYES OF SOMEONE WHO IS LISTENING OR SPEAKING TO YOU

Attention is the most valuable thing you can give to someone. If your goal is to win friends and influence people, give them your full attention.

Easiest way to show it: maintain eye contact.

This doesn't mean you stare down a person without blinking. It means you look at people while they're talking and while you're talking to them (for groups of people, look at each person for a few seconds if you can. For super-large groups, do for a few what you wish you could do for all).

People feel valued when they have your full attention. And they should. Look at how many other things we could be doing with our eyes at the exact moment!

13 BE WELCOMING AND TOLERANT OF PEOPLE WHO HAVE DIFFERENT WAYS OF DOING THINGS.

The one, two or five ways you know of doing things are not the only ways of doing them.

This applies even if you've had what you consider to be success with your methods. Always be open to other ways of doing things.

You never know where a great idea may come from, even if the idea isn't for the current challenge or project. You can only receive when you're open to receiving!

14 ASK PEOPLE QUESTIONS ABOUT THE THINGS THEY CARE ABOUT MOST.

We call these "hot buttons."

Hot buttons are the topics people are most passionate about, topics someone will go on and on about. Though you may end up hearing more than you wanted to, the person talking will have a new friend in you who lets them talk about what they care about.

Value this skill!

15 SEE THE POSITIVE AND POTENTIAL IN EVERYONE YOU MEET.

Every person has potential to improve who they are and what they do, and in turn get better results. Notice this in everyone.

If you don't see it, look for it!

16 WHEN YOU'RE FEELING A LACK OF SOMETHING - MOTIVATION, ENCOURAGEMENT, IDEAS - HELP SOMEONE ELSE BY GIVING THAT EXACT THING TO THEM.

If you want to get money, help someone else get money. -
Russell Simmons

Whatever you need or want in life, set karma in motion for you by helping someone else obtain it.

Want to be happy? Share a smile.

Want to make more money? Empower someone else to make more money.

Want to get motivated? Motivate someone else.

20 LEARN SOME BASIC, CLEAN JOKES THAT YOU CAN USE ANYWHERE AND THAT WILL RELAX PEOPLE.

This is a critical skill when you're introducing yourself to a new group of people, or when you're trying to get everyone on the same page.

People relax when they laugh. They loosen up and find at least one thing in common with others: The humor in the joke.

Simply use Google to find some good jokes that are **not** sexual, racial or political in nature. Don't have a joke alienate anyone in your audience.

21 DEFER TO OTHERS - HOLD DOORS, LET THE OTHER DRIVER GO FIRST, ALLOW THEM THE LAST WORD.

True power does not need to flex its muscle in every little situation and interaction. Beating people to the spot in a merge lane does not show toughness (though it might be fun at times).

You don't have to win every argument. Stop trying to dominate every conversation.

22 SHARE STORIES OF YOUR OWN SETBACKS AND FAILURES.

Great as you may be, you are not perfect. It is dangerous to be held up as someone without failings - envious people will seek and find them for you, if you don't first.

Make a show of your own deficiencies. It can be something small and benign, but make it something that shows you're not some infallible statue with no flaws.

This open vulnerability endears you to your listeners and makes it safe for them to do the same.

23 RESPECT OTHERS' PERSPECTIVES, EVEN WHEN YOU DISAGREE.

You will not see things the same way as every person you meet or converse with.

But you can still agree with them.

Huh? What?

When someone offers an opinion or idea that you differ with, you can agree by understanding their perspective.

Mr. Salesman, this car costs too much!

I understand how you feel, Mr. Prospect. Take a look at this...

So you can understand why and how people feel how they feel while still having your own opinion. This is especially true if you're working to get agreement with someone. You won't get agreement by disagreeing with people.

24 ASK QUESTIONS OF PEOPLE WHOSE VIEWS CONFLICT WITH YOURS - WITH AN INTENTION OF LEARNING.

After agreeing with your counterpart's perspective, your next step is to learn.

Ask questions, shut up and listen.

Find out how she came to her conclusion. You might learn something that you didn't know, like a different way of seeing the same information. And the person you're talking to can still become an ally because you haven't offended her or made her an enemy by arguing.

25 BE PATIENT.

Rushing leads to stress and anxiety. Stress and anxiety kill people before their time. Don't become the next victim. Learn patience.

There are actions you can take that will help you develop more patience.

Develop a feeling of confidence that tells you that everything is going to happen exactly when and how it needs to happen.

Take deep breaths more often. Down into your belly.

Plan to do things early - assignments, waking up, getting to the airport, filing paperwork - so you're not rushing at the last minute.

26 SHOW AND ORALLY EXPRESS TRUST IN PEOPLE BEFORE THEY HAVE DEMONSTRATED IT.

Trust is a self-fulfilling prophecy. When you tell someone "I trust you," you increase the chances that he does (or doesn't do) what you're entrusting him to do (or not do). The statement itself is a verbal contract of sorts that anchors someone to the stated agreement.

Orally stating it also puts the "trustworthy" title on a person, which increases the chances she acts in a manner reflective of the title.

27 PUT YOURSELF IN SOMEONE ELSE'S SHOES.

Don't be so quick to judge other people. No matter how much you think you know someone, you will never know everything about them.

Have you ever had things going on in your life that you didn't share with people close to you? Of course you have. Which means you know other people do the same. The person you're judging may be going through a hardship that they would never tell you about. And frankly, it may be none of your business anyway.

If you feel you need to know what's going on with someone, such as a spouse, teammate or coworker, do the only smart thing: Ask questions. Be open and friendly and empathetic when doing so, not accusatory or probing.

Then shut up and listen.

28 BE FLEXIBLE.

Sure, you have your ideas, beliefs, and ways of doing things, as everyone does.

You have some hardened stereotypes in your mind that you will not let go of, no matter how nonsensical they are, no matter how much logic gets put in front of you. And you're damn good at defending yourself when they get questioned.

My advice is, the fewer of these you have, the better.

Overall, push yourself to open your mind more. Accept that your way of thinking, doing and being is neither the "right" way nor the only way.

Accept the differences of other people as best you can (your "best" in this area should always be expanding).

At work, be able to adjust on the fly anytime you're not the one calling the shots. Change will happen whether you like it or not, and things will move on with or without you.

29 BE OPEN-MINDED.

Be willing to consider new ideas.

Welcome new people.

Accept and move with change as it happens.

Never close your mind off to something you don't know anything about.

This doesn't mean you have to *do* everything, but don't assume you know things when you know you don't.

30 THINK HOW WE CAN INSTEAD OF WHY WE CAN'T.

Thinking *how we can* asks your mind to develop solutions and ideas. It's a starting point of thinking and creativity. People who always appear to create something out of nothing are *how we can* thinkers.

Why we can't is a finishing point. It's a mindset that there is nothing more to be considered or thought about or done. Its definitive and a closed door to creativity.

31 BE OPEN ABOUT YOUR IGNORANCE.

Ignorance is when you don't know something. You are uninformed, uneducated, seeing something you have no experience in.

When you're looking at or experiencing something new, ignorance is expected. So be open about it.

You don't need to pretend like you do know something that you don't know and wouldn't be expected to know.

If someone expects you to know something that you don't know, you'll have to decide which is better: admitting you don't know and learning, or pretending you do know and messing everything up as a result? If you don't know, don't you think it will be obvious before long?

Learn to ask questions (see a theme in this book?) when you don't know stuff. Admit that you don't know, and ask someone who does. Usually they will be happy to educate you and show off their smarts. Give them the chance.

32 LISTEN TO OR READ 15 MINUTES MINIMUM OF POSITIVE, UPLIFTING PERSONAL DEVELOPMENT MATERIAL.

15 minutes is a **minimum** for those of you who just want to get by. If you're serious, an hour is your low-end day.

Personal development is any material that will make you smarter, a better worker, more valuable in the marketplace, easier to get along with, or a better generator of ideas. Personal development can be found in books, podcasts, audio tapes, seminars, coaching, and classes (online or in-person).

Personal development, when used consistently, requires you to think critically and make changes in your life.

What Personal development is NOT:

* Reality Television

* Music - singing, rapping etc

* Movies

If you're serious about doing better with people, get your personal development in daily. Require it of yourself the same way you require eating or brushing your teeth.

33 REMAIN CALM WHEN OTHERS ARE REACTIVE, ANGRY OR NERVOUS.

When emotions are running high, the leader is the one who maintains his sense of self. The leader can see clearly when everyone else's vision is clouded by uncontrolled energy.

34 DON'T ALLOW ANYONE TO FEEL LEFT OUT OF THE GROUP.

This is for the Leaders.

When you're leading a group, everyone in the group should feel welcome, needed and a part of what's going on. It's your job to make sure this energy exists.

35 ASK PEOPLE FOR FEEDBACK ON HOW YOU CAN GET BETTER.

No one is too good to stop getting better. When that happens, you're fitting yourself for a casket.

Seek feedback from others on how you can improve. Not just from the experts and people who are ahead of you, either.

Ask people who know *nothing* about your line of work what their impression is of what you do. You will receive insightful comments.

Even if you know nothing about basketball, you could watch a game and tell who the best players are.

I don't have to know the finer points of speaking to tell if a presenter got her point across powerfully.

Make sure the people you ask are people who are comfortable telling you when you suck. Feedback from people who need you to be happy with them is useless.

Always look for ways you can get better. That's the only way it will ever happen.

36 GO A STEP DEEPER IN CASUAL CONVERSATION WITH PEOPLE.

Learn to listen and ask questions based on what you hear - what is said and what is *not* said. Ask people things they have not been asked before (you won't know you did until they tell you).

How do you do that? Go off the normal path of questions that *you* get asked all the time. Pay attention. Be more interested in the other person than you are in what you're going to say next.

37 MAKE LIGHTHEARTED JOKES ABOUT YOURSELF TO NOT APPEAR TOO PERFECT.

Making light of yourself lets people know that you don't take yourself so seriously. People will relax around you and be more willing to share things about themselves.

38 TALK HIGHLY OF PEOPLE WITH FRAGILE EGOS - ESPECIALLY IN FRONT OF OTHERS.

Publicly compliment someone who isn't as confident as you are.

Make them feel important in front of a group.

Make sure what you say is genuine and based on something they are or have done.

39 NEVER LINGER FOR TOO LONG.

This applies to conversation as well as your physical presence.

Better to be missed than to be overbearing.

Where have you been? Is a better question than *why are you still here?*

40 LET THE OTHER PERSON TALK MORE THAN YOU.

Two common themes in this book are asking questions and listening. If you've read this far, then this skill should come easy to you.

Just remember: **People care more about themselves than they care about you.**

41 PAINT BEAUTIFUL PICTURES OF THE FUTURE.

Great leaders aren't necessarily the ones who have all the answers or even the right answers.

Most great leaders who you can name are great at painting pictures. Pictures of what the future holds, what things will look like, how great life will be. We like following these people because everyday life is not nearly as exciting as the possibilities a leader shares.

Pictures of the future get people interested and excited. People will follow you when you develop this skill. Following you and your vision releases a person from the boring monotony of his everyday life.

42 DON'T TALK TOO MUCH ABOUT YOUR SPECIFIC PLANS.

There are a few reasons for this.

1. People care more about *their* own plans than yours.

2. No one needs to know exactly what you're up to all the time.

3. Talking about what you're going to do is not nearly as exciting as doing it.

4. We don't believe much of what we hear. Seeing is self-evident.

43 AVOID ARGUMENT AT ALL COST.

A man convinced against his will is of the same opinion still.

Arguing doesn't win you agreement or friends. Argument can, however, alienate people, create enemies and ensure that someone will never open up to you again.

Knowing this, it would seem that we would never argue. It's in the heat of a conversation, when we have no time to consult logic, that it happens.

What you can do, then, is to become aware of your own internal thermometer when you feel argument coming on. Identify your own energy, **find agreement with others,** and let it go.

If you are indeed correct about the topic - and come on, we *know* you are - then time and experience will prove it for you.

44 TALK ABOUT WHAT THE OTHER PERSON IS INTERESTED IN.

Newsflash: This is probably not what *you're* interested in. And that's ok. Because your goal is to get better with other people, not with yourself.

45 MEET AS MANY PEOPLE AS POSSIBLE.

I don't see any drawbacks to knowing more people and having more people know you.

They can connect you to other people, share valuable information, refer you business, and help you out when you need it.

You can leverage their time, money, energy, knowledge and the people they know.

And if you're ever in an online poll, they can vote for you.

46 AVOID POLITICS AND RELIGION AS DISCUSSION TOPICS.

Now, politics and religion *are* hot button topics. But they are also very divisive hot button topics, the type of topics that I have never seen anyone change stance on as a result of a conversation.

Have you ever seen a Christian persuaded to turn Jewish at a networking event?

What about a Republican switching over to Democrat because of someone's strong liberal viewpoints?

Anyone who has these hot buttons surely has others. Make it your job to find those others and leave politics and religion alone.

47 MAKE OTHERS FEEL SMARTER THAN YOU.

Robert Greene covers this in depth in *The 48 Laws of Power*.

Of the many ways one person can demonstrate superiority over others - physical strength, finances, beauty - intelligence is the one area in which the offended is least forgiving. Even worse, they will never tell you so, creating a silent enemy.

So if you're a really intelligent person, learn to sometimes dull your colors around others, especially those who you find to be insecure.

You do this by simply shutting up (you can't show off your brilliance when you're not talking) and listening. Speak only to ask questions.

48 ALWAYS ASK PERMISSION BEFORE OFFERING FEEDBACK.

Unsolicited opinion and advice is probably the least-wanted type of dialogue known to man.

But what if you really know a lot and you want to help someone? Should you just not help them?

Here's what you do: Ask.

Hey, I loved your speech. Would it be ok if I shared some constructive feedback with you?

Great game yesterday! You are one of the best I've seen this season. Could I offer you something I noticed about your style of play?

Most people would happily say yes to this.

Try it yourself. Never push your opinions and advice on someone who did not ask for or agree to receiving it.

49 ALWAYS GIVE MORE THAN YOU GET.

What you put out, you get back. If you agree with this, then you should be stuffing your karma bank account with as many deposits as you can.

Help other people. Motivate them, tell someone something good, bring positive energy to what you do. The universe will pay you back when it balances everything out.

Give more than you get, and you will have legions of people wanting to help you in return. These people will not necessarily be the same people you have helped. Just the law of karma in action.

50 DISPLAY YOUR SIMILARITIES WITH OTHERS TO BUILD RAPPORT.

Find common ground with people. No matter how small that ground, you can build on it and develop a relationship.

Common ground lets another person say, *she's just like me!* We trust, identify with and do business with people who are like us.

If you and another person are talking, you have something in common. Even if it's nothing more than the fact that you both are in that conversation at the moment.

51 KNOW HOW FAR YOU CAN GO WITH PEOPLE.

Jokes. Prodding. Motivating.

Every human being has a breaking point.

You are much better off stopping short of that breaking point than you are in going too far.

52 ASK SOMEONE FOR HELP.

All humans yearn for power on some level. This is one way to give it to them.

Asking someone for help puts them in a position of power: They can do or answer something for you that you (seemingly) cannot for yourself.

Contrary to popular belief, asking for help does not make you weak. It empowers people.

53 SHARE FREELY WITH OTHERS.

Ideas. Knowledge. Information. Energy. Motivation.

When you have them, share them with others. You can create more of all of that stuff anyway. It's not a zero-sum game.

You know what I said earlier about karma. Get it working for you.

Give until they can't live without you. - Russell Simmons

54 EXERCISE THE SKILL OF SAYING NO FIRMLY.

No.

The easiest and the hardest word to say.

When your answers really is No, say it firmly and leave no loopholes for further possibilities.

Which means, no explanation of why you're saying No and no contingencies for turning the No into a Yes.

55 ENJOY PEOPLE.

I mean, *really* enjoy people.

See the possibilities in others.

Know that no matter how much you know, you still know very little about other people. Fill that knowledge gap by asking questions.

ABOUT DRE BALDWIN

Dre Baldwin is the world's only expert on Mental Toughness, Confidence and Self-Discipline. A 9-year professional basketball player, Dre works with athletes, entrepreneurs and business professionals.

Dre has worked with Nike, Finish Line, Wendy's Gatorade, Buick, Wilson Sports and DIME magazine.

Dre has been blogging since 2005 and started publishing to YouTube in 2006. He has over 5,000 videos published, with daily content going out to his 115,000+ subscribers and being viewed over 35 million times. Dre's "Work On Your Game" show on Grant Cardone TV is consistently top-5 in views on the network.

Dre speaks, coaches and consults business professionals on mental toughness, confidence and discipline. He has given 3 TED Talks, published 7 books and has a daily podcast, Work On Your Game with DreAllDay. A Philadelphia native and Penn State alum, Dre lives in Miami.

Twitter & Periscope

@DreAllDay

Instagram, SnapChat & SoundCloud

@DreBaldwin

READ MORE BY DRE BALDWIN,
INCLUDING:

Buy A Game
The Mental Handbook
Mirror Of Motivation
The Super You
The Overseas Basketball
Blueprint
Dre Philosophy Vol. 0
100 Mental Game Best Practices
25 Conversation Starters

Made in the USA
Columbia, SC
10 January 2022

52777204R00050